General Knowledge Olympiad

Class 01

A must have book for all
Olympiads & Talent Search Exams...

by
Taru Kaushik

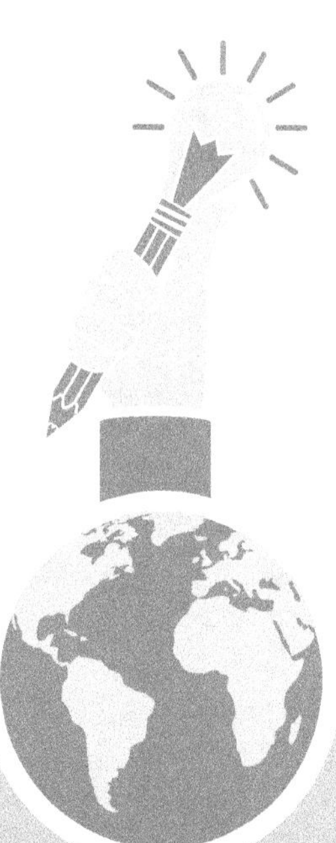

BLoOM CAP
Bloom Cap Edu Ventures Pvt. Ltd.

Bloom Cap Edu Ventures Pvt. Ltd.

Administrative & Production Office

'Ramchhaya' 4577/15, Agarwal Road, Darya Ganj, New Delhi -110002
Tele: 011- 47630600, 43518550

ISBN : 978-93-25519-40-4

PRICE : ₹100.00

PO No : TXT-XX-XXXXXXX-X-XX

For further information about the books log on to
www.bloomcap.org

Follow us on   

Preface

"Future belongs to those Who prepares for it today"

School Olympiads are National & International level competitions conducted by different Government, Non-Government & Educational Organisations with the purpose of making the children ready to face competitive exams.

The challenging Questions asked in Olympiads motivate them to learn more & more and bring out the best result with improved academic performance. The Awards & Scholarship offered by Olympiads motivate children to aspire & strive for doing better and emerge out to be the best.

GK Olympiads

GK is the knowledge of every aspect of the human life, which may or may not be the part of routine academic studies but very important for the overall personality development of the students. It is more or less connected with the attentiveness and awareness. There can be different domains of GK like; History, Geography, Polity, Culture, Discovery, Sports, Current Affairs etc.

GK Olympiads help students in understanding the importance of General Knowledge and updations about National & International Affairs in daily life..

'Bloom GK Olympiad Study Book Class 1' is a perfect resource to Study & Practice for Olympiad Exams and other National & State Level Talent Search Exams & Other Competitions.

Some Special Features of Bloom GK Olympiad Study Books are;

- Complete coverage of all the topics related to GK;. History, Geography, Environment, Polity, Culture, Sports, Current Affairs etc.
- Chapterwise Exercises having different types of Objective Questions.
- Olympiad Pattern Practice Sets at the end.

This book is prepared by Expert Panel with the utmost care, still if you have any suggestions regarding its improvement then feel free to contact us at olympiads@bloomcap.org. We will try to inculcate your suggestions in the further editions.

Contents

Chapter 01

Me and My Family

1. Who among the following is not a family member?
   (a) Brother
   (b) Mother
   (c) Grandfather
   (d) Friends

2. If Sophie is the only sibling of James. It means James has........... .
   (a) one friend
   (b) one brother
   (c) one sister
   (d) one pet

3. Seema has two brothers and one sister. How many siblings does she have?
   (a) 1
   (b) 3
   (c) 4
   (d) 5

4. What is your relation with your father's mother?
   (a) Aunt
   (b) Grandmother
   (c) Mother
   (d) Sister

5. What is your relation with your mother's brother?
   (a) Maternal uncle
   (b) Nephew
   (c) Niece
   (d) Cousin

6. Your uncle Rajesh has only one son, Rahul. What is relation with Rahul?
   (a) Nephew
   (b) Cousin
   (c) Niece
   (d) Son

7. Find the odd one out.
   (a) Grandfather – Grandmother
   (b) Father – Mother
   (c) Uncle – Aunt
   (d) Brother – Sister

8. Rohan living with his wife and two children. Which type of family does Rohan have?
   (a) Big family
   (b) Small family
   (c) Joint family
   (d) None of these

9. There are six members in Robin's family. His grandparents, parents and one sister. Who is the head of the family?
(a) Father
(b) Mother
(c) Sister
(d) Grandfather

10. Garima is your mother's sister. How is Garima related to you?
(a) Cousin
(b) Maternal aunt
(c) Niece
(d) Parental aunt

11. Match the following.

List I		List II
A. Maternal aunt	1.	Grandmother's husband
B. Parental aunt	2.	Father's son
C. Brother	3.	Father's sister
D. Grandfather	4.	Mother's sister

Codes

	A	B	C	D			A	B	C	D
(a)	4	3	2	1		(b)	2	3	4	1
(c)	3	4	1	2		(d)	1	2	3	4

12. Which one of the following family members are there in the joint family?
(a) Parents
(b) Siblings
(c) Grandparents
(d) All of these

13. John and George are my uncle's children. How they are related to me?
(a) They are my cousins
(b) They are my brothers
(c) They are my friends
(d) They are my uncle

14. Which one of the following is not correctly matched?
(a) Uncle's daughter – Niece
(b) Uncle's wife – Aunt
(c) Mother's father – Grandfather
(d) Grandmother's husband – Grandfather

15. Seema is going to her mother's home. She will not find her .... there.
(a) maternal uncle
(b) maternal aunt
(c) maternal grandfather
(d) parental grandmother

16. If I live with my parents and two siblings in Delhi, how many members are there in my family?
(a) Five
(b) Six
(c) Four
(d) Two

17. The grandson of your grandparent's is your............ .
  (a) brother   (b) son
  (c) father   (d) None of these

18. Find ''X''. If ''X'' is your brother's son, how ''X'' is related to you?
  (a) Niece   (b) Nephew
  (c) Cousin   (d) Maternal uncle

19. The picture given depicts which type of family?

  (a) Small family   (b) Big family
  (c) Joint family   (d) None of these

20. Our parental uncle is ....
  (a) father's brother   (b) grandfather's son
  (c) mother's brother   (d) Both (a) and (b)

21. Mother of your mother is your ....
  (a) grandmother   (b) niece
  (c) mother   (d) maternal grandfather

22. On the occasion of Rakshabandhan, who will come to your home to tie Rakhi to your father?
  (a) Your maternal aunt   (b) Your sister
  (c) Your parental aunt   (d) Your niece

Our Surroundings

1. Ram wants to post a letter to his friend. Where he will go to post the letter?
   (a) Police station
   (b) Hospital
   (c) Post office
   (d) School

2. Why we go to the hospital?
   (a) Doctor treats us when we are not well
   (b) To study
   (c) To buy furniture
   (d) To play

3. A place where children go to study and learn many new things is a ....
   (a) Police station
   (b) Restaurants
   (c) School
   (d) Market

4. Which one of the following things you will not find in park?
   (a) Books
   (b) Swings
   (c) Chairs
   (d) Playing grounds

5. The given tool is used by which of the following?

   (a) Blacksmith
   (b) Teacher
   (c) Mason
   (d) Carpenter

6. If cobbler uses leather, writer uses pen, carpenter will use ....
   (a) Books
   (b) Wood
   (c) Mobile Phone
   (d) Hammer

7. Who makes food in a restaurant?
(a) Farmer
(b) Cook/Chef
(c) Baker
(d) Gardener

8. Match the following.

	List I		List II
A.	Teaches us in school	1.	Carpenter
B.	Paint our house	2.	Potter
C.	Make furniture	3.	Painter
D.	Make earthern pots	4.	Teacher

Codes

	A	B	C	D			A	B	C	D
(a)	2	3	4	1		(b)	4	3	1	2
(c)	4	3	2	1		(d)	1	2	3	4

9. Which one of the following sells medicines and injections?
(a) Tailor
(b) Painter
(c) Chemist
(d) Nurse

10. Which one of the following guards our country on border?
(a) Watchman
(b) Doctor
(c) Policeman
(d) Army soldiers

11. Find the odd one out.
(a) Hospital
(b) School
(c) Library
(d) Principal

12. A person who stitches our clothes is known as ....
(a) tailor
(b) carpenter
(c) gardener
(d) dentist

13. We go to .... to worship Jesus Christ.
(a) mosque
(b) gurudwara
(c) temple
(d) church

14. Where will you go to buy everyday things like bread, butter, fruits and vegetables?
(a) Library
(b) Hospital
(c) Market
(d) Park

15. Which one of the following is not correctly matched?
(a) Police station- to study
(b) Park- to play and to do walk
(c) Library- to borrow and to read the books
(d) Temple - to worship the God

16. A .... grows crops, fruit and vegetables for us in fields.
    (a) fireman
    (b) gardener
    (c) farmer
    (d) blacksmith

17. Who fits water taps and pipes at our home?
    (a) Mason
    (b) Plumber
    (c) Carpenter
    (d) Teacher

18. .... helps us in catching thieves and keeping our neighbourhood safe.
    (a) Policeman
    (b) Teacher
    (c) Gardener
    (d) Scientist

19. To whom will you call when you see fire in your neighbourhood?
    (a) Fire station
    (b) Police station
    (c) Ambulance
    (d) Post office

20. Which one of the following cares for our gardens?
    (a) Nurse
    (b) Gatekeeper
    (c) Mason
    (d) Gardener

Good Habits and Manners

1. From the given options, which one is a bad habit?
   (a) To put your toys into a box after playing
   (b) Arrange books on the table after studying
   (c) Putting clothes and dresses in almirah
   (d) Eating food while laying down on bed

2. Which of the following activities should be done once in a week?
   (a) Comb the hair
   (b) Brush your teeth
   (c) Take bath
   (d) Cutting nails

3. Which one of the following is a good habit?
   (a) Fighting with friends
   (b) Throw garbage in dustbin
   (c) Shouting in public place
   (d) Making paintings on school wall

4. From the given options, identify the person who is performing a good habit.
   (a) Ram-During school prayer, I remain in the class.
   (b) Naina-I clean my nose by curtains.
   (c) Rohit- I flush the toilet everytime I use it.
   (d) Seema-I throw stones on street dogs.

5. Which of the following activities should we practice in school?
   (a) Climb on desk and play with friends
   (b) Respect your teachers
   (c) Don't listen to your teacher
   (d) Come late to school

6. When we must wash our hands?
   (a) Before taking meal
   (b) After taking meal
   (c) Never
   (d) Both (a) and (b)

7. Which of the following we must do when we meet with someone?
   (a) Ignore them
   (b) Shake hands with them
   (c) Exchange greetings and pleasantries
   (d) Both (b) and (c)

8. Which one of the following activities should be done to stay fit and healthy?
   - (a) Play and exercise
   - (b) Maintain a good body posture
   - (c) Take good sleep for eight hours a day
   - (d) All of these

9. Which one of the following is not a good manner?
   - (a) Respect your elders
   - (b) Fight with younger brothers and sisters
   - (c) Listen to parents carefully
   - (d) Pray to God

10. Which of the following is a bad manner while eating food?
    - (a) We should use spoons and plates
    - (b) We should chew the food slowly
    - (c) We should not talk while eating
    - (d) We should scatter food on the table

11. Which one of the following is a good manner while travelling on the road?
    - (a) Bicycling faster on the roads
    - (b) Split on the road
    - (c) Help an elderly person in crossing the road
    - (d) Throw packets on the road after eating

12. Which one of the following is not a good manner while going to friend's home?
    - (a) Knock the door before entering
    - (b) Wish their parents
    - (c) Shout and play inside the house
    - (d) Sit gently in their home

13. Which one of the following is a good manner when living in your home?
    - (a) Help your mother in small works
    - (b) Help small sister in studying
    - (c) Sit with grandparents and respect them
    - (d) All of these

14. Which one of the following activities we must do when we speak or talk with someone?
    - (a) Listen to them carefully
    - (b) Interrupt when they are speaking
    - (c) Wait for your turn to speak
    - (d) Both (a) and (c)

15. How many hours in a day should we atleast sleep to take proper rest?
    - (a) 12 hours in a day
    - (b) 4 hours in a day
    - (c) 8 hours in a day
    - (d) 2 hours in a day

16. Which one of the following is not a good habit while playing in playground?
    - (a) Disturbing others in the ground
    - (b) Play with friends
    - (c) Wait for your turn at the sea-saw
    - (d) Don't fight with others

17. We must cover our mouth when we are ....
    - (a) talking with friends
    - (b) sneezing in public
    - (c) coughing in school
    - (d) Both (b) and (c)

My Country

1. In which of the following years our country got independence?
   (a) 1950
   (b) 1947
   (c) 1948
   (d) 1949

2. Which city is called the Queen of Hills?
   (a) Delhi
   (b) Shimla
   (c) Ooty
   (d) Jaipur

3. Which city is located on sea coast?
   (a) Bangalore
   (b) Kanpur
   (c) Mumbai
   (d) Bhopal

4. Find the odd one out from the given options.
   (a) Uttar Pradesh
   (b) Madhya Pradesh
   (c) Bihar
   (d) Puducherry

5. Identify "X". People in state "X" wears Turban on their head. The Bhangra dance is also famous in state X.
   (a) Punjab
   (b) Karnataka
   (c) Kerala
   (d) Tamil Nadu

6. Match the following.

States	Capitals
A. Tamil Nadu	1. Mumbai
B. Maharashtra	2. Gandhinagar
C. West Bengal	3. Chennai
D. Gujarat	4. Kolkata

Codes

	A	B	C	D			A	B	C	D
(a)	1	2	3	4		(b)	4	3	2	1
(c)	3	1	4	2		(d)	2	3	4	1

7. Which state has the smallest number of people living in it?
(a) Uttar Pradesh
(b) Goa
(c) Sikkim
(d) Bihar

8. Match the following.

List I	List II
A. Northern State	1. Arunachal Pradesh
B. Southern State	2. Gujarat
C. Eastern State	3. Tamil Nadu
D. Western State	4. Jammu and Kashmir

Codes

	A	B	C	D			A	B	C	D
(a)	3	4	1	2		(b)	4	3	1	2
(c)	4	3	2	1		(d)	1	2	3	4

9. Find the odd one out.
(a) Daman and Diu
(b) Gujarat
(c) West Bengal
(d) Uttar Pradesh

10. In the given options, names of states and capitals are given. Find out the name of capital.
(a) Assam
(b) Odisha
(c) Bhopal
(d) Chhattisgarh

11. How many union territories are there in our country?
(a) 7
(b) 8
(c) 9
(d) 10

12. Which one of the following is not a hilly area?
(a) Jammu and Kashmir
(b) Himachal Pradesh
(c) Arunachal Pradesh
(d) Uttar Pradesh

13. Which among the following is the biggest state of India?
(a) Rajasthan
(b) Himachal Pradesh
(c) Goa
(d) New Delhi

14. Lucknow is the capital of the state ....
(a) Uttar Pradesh
(b) Assam
(c) Sikkim
(d) Himachal Pradesh

15. Which one of the following is known as pink city?
    (a) Jaipur   (b) Prayagraj
    (c) Bhubaneswar   (d) Mumbai

16. Haridwar and Rishikesh are the famous cities located in which of the following states?
    (a) Uttarakhand   (b) Goa
    (c) Jammu and Kashmir   (d) Punjab

17. Which of the following states is not surrounded with the ocean?
    (a) Madhya Pradesh   (b) Tamil Nadu
    (c) Kerala   (d) Karnataka

18. Surat and Gandhinagar are cities of which state?
    (a) Uttar Pradesh   (b) Rajasthan
    (c) Gujarat   (d) Maharashtra

19. Which one of the following is not a name of Union Territory of India?
    (a) Puducherry   (b) Lakshadweep
    (c) Sikkim   (d) Jammu and Kashmir

20. Which of the following states is not located in the Northern part of India?
    (a) Punjab   (b) Haryana
    (c) Himachal Pradesh   (d) Maharashtra

21. Which one of the following famous hill station is not located in Uttarakhand?
    (a) Mussoorie   (b) Rishikesh
    (c) Shimla   (d) Lansdowne

22. If Kolkata is known as City of Joy, then Udaipur is known as ....
    (a) City of Lakes   (b) Pink City
    (c) Orange City   (d) Diamond City

23. Which one of the following places is known as ''Heaven on Earth''?
    (a) Punjab   (b) Kashmir
    (c) Chhattisgarh   (d) Bihar

Chapter

05

Our National Symbols

1. Which among the following is our national water animal?
   (a) Snake   (b) Fish
   (c) Ostrich   (d) Dolphin

2. How many colour strips are there in our national flag?
   (a) 1   (b) 2
   (c) 3   (d) 4

3. What is the duration of our national anthem 'JANA GANA MANA'?
   (a) 50 seconds   (b) 51 seconds
   (c) 52 seconds   (d) 60 seconds

4. Which one of these is not correctly matched?
   (a) National Fruit –   Mango   (b) National Flower –   Rose
   (c) National Bird   –   Peacock   (d) National Animal –   Tiger

5. Which one of the following colours is not present in our national flag?
   (a) Red   (b) Green
   (c) White   (d) Saffron

6. Vande Mataram is our ....
   (a) National Anthem   (b) National Song
   (c) National Emblem   (d) National Movie

7. Which currency has been shown in the picture given below?

   (a) Rupee   (b) Dollar
   (c) Pound   (d) Yen

8. The given image was adopted as our .... on 26th January, 1950.

सत्यमेव जयते

   (a) National sign   (b) National Emblem
   (c) National Anthem   (d) National logo

9. Which one of the following flowers is considered as our national Flower?
   (a) Lotus   (b) Rose
   (c) Lily   (d) Marigold

10. Which one of the following is considered as our national heritage animal?
   (a) Elephant   (b) Giraffe
   (c) Zebra   (d) Leopard

11. Which one of the following rivers is considered as our national river?
   (a) Ganga   (b) Yamuna
   (c) Saraswati   (d) Godavari

12. Which among the following is our national motto?
   (a) Do or Die   (b) Satyamev Jayate
   (c) We are Indian   (d) Sare Jahan se Accha

13. Our National Emblem was taken from ....
   (a) lion capital of Ashoka at Sarnath   (b) lion capital of Akbar at Allahabad
   (c) lion capital of Shah Jahan at Agra   (d) None of these

14. How many spokes are present in the wheel present in the centre of our national flag?
   (a) 20   (b) 21
   (c) 22   (d) 24

15. Which one of the following is considered as our national tree?
   (a) Neem tree   (b) Banyan tree
   (c) Tulsi tree   (d) Ashoka tree

Our Freedom Fighters and National Leaders

1. Which among the following is known as 'Father of Nation'?
   (a) Dr. A.P.J Abdul Kalam
   (b) Mahatma Gandhi
   (c) Jawaharlal Nehru
   (d) Rabindranath Tagore

2. .... is also known as 'Neta ji'.
   (a) Jawaharlal Nehru
   (b) Mahatma Gandhi
   (c) Sardar Vallabhbhai Patel
   (d) Subhash Chandra Bose

3. Identify the personality shown in the picture.

   (a) Jawaharlal Nehru
   (b) Mahatma Gandhi
   (c) Bal Gangadhar Tilak
   (d) Sardar Vallabhbhai Patel

4. Identify the freedom fighter shown in the picture.

   (a) Rani Mira Bai
   (b) Rani Lakshmi Bai
   (c) Sarojini Naidu
   (d) Vijaya Laxmi Pandit

5. Which one of the following personalities called himself 'Azad'?
   (a) Mahatma Gandhi
   (b) Subhas Chandra Bose
   (c) Chandra Shekar
   (d) Bhagat Singh

6. Which of the following was not a freedom fighter?
   (a) Rani Lakshmi Bai
   (b) Mangal Pandey
   (c) Mahatma Gandhi
   (d) Tantia Tope

7. Which of the following freedom fighters got hanged together?
   (a) Bhagat Singh
   (b) Rajguru
   (c) Sukhdev
   (d) All of these

8. What was the name of the freedom fighter who shot himself in the head?
   (a) Chandra Shekhar Azad
   (b) Bhagat Singh
   (c) Mahatma Gandhi
   (d) Jawaharlal Nehru

9. Which of the following personalities is also known as 'Chacha Nehru'?
   (a) Jawaharlal Nehru
   (b) Mahatma Gandhi
   (c) Rabindranath Tagore
   (d) Swami Vivekananda

10. Identify the given personality.

   (a) B.R. Ambedkar
   (b) Dayanand Saraswati
   (c) Ruskin Bond
   (d) J.R.D Tata

11. Identify the freedom fighter shown in the picture.

   (a) Sukhdev
   (b) Rajguru
   (c) Bhagat Singh
   (d) Mangal Pandey

12. Which one of the following leaders is also known as 'LOKMANYA'?
    (a) Bal Gangadhar Tilak   (b) Lala Lajpat Rai
    (c) Subhas Chandra Bose   (d) Jawaharlal Nehru

13. Which of the following leaders of India is also known as 'Man of Peace'?
    (a) B.R. Ambedkar   (b) Sardar Vallabhbhai Patel
    (c) Mahatma Gandhi   (d) Lal Bahadur Shastri

14. Mahatma Gandhi is commonly known as......... .
    (a) Neta ji   (b) Bapu
    (c) Shaheed   (d) Gurudev

15. Which of the following gave the slogan 'Aaram haram hai'?
    (a) Sardar Vallabhbhai Patel   (b) Jawaharlal Nehru
    (c) Mahatma Gandhi   (d) Subhas Chandra Bose

16. Which of the following national leaders, dedicated to 'The Statue of Unity'?
    (a) Bhagat Singh   (b) Rajguru
    (c) B.R. Ambedkar   (d) Sardar Patel

17. The freedom fighter shown in the picture gave the slogan – Give me Blood, I shall give you freedom. Who is he?

    (a) Lal Bahadur Shastri   (b) Jawaharlal Nehru
    (c) Subhas Chandra Bose   (d) Mangal Pandey

18. Which one of the following national leaders is also known as Baba Saheb?
    (a) Lal Bahadur Shastri   (b) B.R. Ambedkar
    (c) Chandra Shekhar Azad   (d) Sukhdev

Fairs, Festivals and Religions

1. Which one of the following is our national festival?
   (a) Holi
   (b) Diwali
   (c) Christmas
   (d) Independence Day

2. Which of the following festivals is known as festival of colours?
   (a) Republic Day
   (b) Holi
   (c) Onam
   (d) Diwali

3. In which of the following festivals sisters tie rakhi on the arms of their brothers and wish for health and well being?
   (a) Dusshera
   (b) Guruparva
   (c) Raksha Bandhan
   (d) Christmas

4. Which one of the following is not a national festival of India?
   (a) Dusshera
   (b) Gandhi Jayanti
   (c) Republic Day
   (d) Independence Day

5. Identify the festival shown in the picture given below.

   (a) Diwali
   (c) Christmas
   (c) Good Friday
   (d) Holi

6. In which of the following festivals, people decorate their houses with candles and worship Goddess Lakshmi?

    (a) Diwali

    (b) Holi

    (c) Dusshera

    (d) Bihu

7. In which of the following festivals our muslim friends offer 'Namaz'?

    (a) Eid

    (b) Guruparva

    (c) Dusshera

    (d) Diwali

8. The famous Kumbh Mela is celebrated in which of the following places?

    (a) Haridwar

    (b) Ujjain

    (c) Prayagraj

    (d) All of these

9. Which festival is shown in the picture given below.

    (a) Diwali

    (b) Dusshera

    (c) Kumbh

    (d) Eid

10. Identify the festival shown in the picture. It is celebrated with full joy in Punjab.

    (a) Bihu

    (b) Lohri

    (c) Pongal

    (d) Diwali

11. The famous fair Kumbh Mela is held after how many years?

    (a) 1 year

    (b) 2 years

    (c) 10 years

    (d) 12 years

12. In which of the following festivals our national flag is hoisted by Prime Minister at the Red Fort?

    (a) Gandhi Jayanti

    (b) Independence Day

    (c) Republic Day

    (d) Guruparva

13. Which of the following states hosts the Surajkund Craft mela every year?
    (a) Haryana   (b) Punjab
    (c) Uttar Pradesh   (d) Jammu and Kashmir

14. Which national festival is celebrated on the birth anniversary of the Father of Nation?
    (a) Gurupurab   (b) Independence Day
    (c) Gandhi Jayanti   (d) Republic Day

15. Which of the following festivals is celebrated for 9 days to worship Lord Durga?
    (a) Navratri   (b) Christmas   (c) Eid   (d) Holi

16. The festival Basant Panchmi is dedicated to which of the following?
    (a) Lord Surya   (b) Goddess Saraswati
    (c) Goddess Durga   (d) Lord Shiva

17. Which one of the following is/are religion(s) of India?
    (a) Hinduism   (b) Jainism   (c) Christian   (d) All of these

18. Which one of the following is the biggest religion in India?
    (a) Christian   (b) Muslim   (c) Sikhs   (d) Hinduism

19. Which religious place is shown in the picture given below.

    (a) Temple   (b) Church   (c) Gurudwara   (d) Mosque

20. People of which religion pray to Lord Jesus?
    (a) Hindu   (b) Muslim
    (c) Sikh   (d) Christian

21. Which one of the following goes to Gurudwaras for worshipping?
    (a) Jains   (b) Muslims
    (c) Sikhs   (d) Hindus

22. Which of the following festivals is celebrated as the birth of Lord Krishna?
    (a) Janmashtami   (b) Christmas
    (c) Guruparva   (d) Ram Navmi

Dress and Food

1. Which one of the following wear white colour coat?
   (a) Doctor (b) Engineer
   (c) Policeman (d) Teacher

2. Which one of the following is the food of the state Gujarat?
   (a) Dhokla (b) Idli and Sambhar
   (c) Rice (d) Biryani

3. Identify the person with the help of uniform.

   (a) Armyman (b) Teacher (c) Doctor (d) Postman

4. Who among the following wears turban on their head?
   (a) Hindus (b) Muslim (c) Sikhs (d) Jains

5. Which one of the following is not a part of men's dress?
   (a) Bangles (b) Tie (c) Coat (d) Jacket

6. Which one of the following is the famous dish of the state West Bengal?
   (a) Roshogolla (b) Pav Bhaji
   (c) Sambhar (d) Chole Bhature

7. You will find ...., a famous food in Maharashtra.
   (a) Vada Pav (b) Rice (c) Samosa (d) Dhokla

8. Who among the following wear cap as a part of his uniform?
   (a) Policeman   (b) Armyman   (c) Both (a) and (b)   (d) None of these

9. Which of the following is a type of Western dress?
   (a) Saree   (b) Suits   (c) Dhoti-Kurta   (d) Jeans

10. Which type of clothes we wear in winter season?
    (a) Cotton clothes   (b) Woollen clothes
    (c) Simple clothes   (d) Silk clothes

11. Which one of the following is not the traditional dress of women in India?
    (a) Saree   (b) Kurta   (c) Bangles   (d) Shirt

12. The traditional dress shown in the picture is worn in which state?

    (a) Haryana   (b) Rajasthan   (c) Delhi   (d) Panjab

13. The lawyers in India wear which colour coat in courts?
    (a) Pink   (b) White   (c) Green   (d) Black

14. In which of the following states, the given traditional dress is worn?

    (a) Gujarat   (b) Punjab   (c) Madhya Pradesh   (d) Kerala

15. Which one of the following is not a traditional dress?
    (a) Kurta   (b) Saree   (c) Dhoti   (d) Frocks

Famous Buildings and Monuments

1. Which one of the following monument is situated in the state Punjab?
   (a) Jama Masjid
   (b) Golden Temple
   (c) Taj Mahal
   (d) Victorial Memorial

2. The famous Victoria Memorial is located in ....
   (a) Mumbai
   (b) Chennai
   (c) Kolkata
   (d) Jalandhar

3. Pyramids are found in which country?

   (a) India
   (b) Egypt
   (c) America
   (d) None of these

4. The famous Howrah Bridge is located in which state?
   (a) Calcutta
   (b) Delhi
   (c) Mumbai
   (d) Chennai

5. Which one of the following monuments is not located in New Delhi?
   (a) India Gate
   (b) Red Fort
   (c) Gol Gumbaz
   (d) Jama Masjid

6. Madhya Pradesh is famous for which of the following monuments?
   (a) Sanchi Stupa
   (b) Char Minar
   (c) Gol Gumbaz
   (d) Lotus Temple

7. The famous Taj Mahal is located in which among the following cities of Uttar Pradesh?
   (a) Mathura
   (b) Meerut
   (c) Agra
   (d) Lucknow

8. Identify the given monument.

   (a) Qutub Minar   (b) Golden Temple   (c) India Gate   (d) Char Minar

9. Which one of the following is not matched correctly?
     (a) Lotus Temple – New Delhi   (b) Akshardham Temple – Chhattisgarh
     (c) Golden Temple – Punjab   (d) Sanchi Stupa – Madhya Pradesh

10. The given picture is 'Statue of Unity'. It is located in ....

   (a) Gujarat   (b) Jharkhand   (c) Madhya Pradesh   (d) Rajasthan

11. The famous monument Purana qila (old fort) is located in which city?
     (a) Mumbai   (b) Chennai   (c) Delhi   (d) Calcutta

12. Identify the given monument.

   (a) Agra Fort   (b) Jama Masjid   (c) Red Fort   (d) Jantar Mantar

13. The famous Jagannath Temple is located in ....
     (a) Puri, Odisha   (b) Kolkata, West Bengal
     (c) Lucknow, Uttar Pradesh   (d) Indore, Madhya Pradesh

14. Identify the given monument.

(a) Humayun Tomb
(b) Hawa Mahal
(c) Char Minar
(d) None of these

15. Identify the given monument.

(a) Red Fort
(b) Char Minar
(c) Jantar Mantar
(d) Buland Darwaza

16. Which one of the following monuments is also known as "Palace of Winds"?
(a) Rashtrapati Bhawan
(b) Hawa Mahal
(c) Buland Darwaza
(d) Sanchi Stupa

17. The Rock Garden is located in ....
(a) Puducherry
(b) Chandigarh
(c) Lakshadweep
(d) Punjab

18. What is the name of the famous tower given in the picture?

(a) Eiffel Tower
(b) Tower of London
(c) Sky Tower
(d) Statue of Liberty

19. The longest wall "The Great Wall" is located in which of the following countries?
    (a) Pakistan   (b) Brazil
    (c) China   (d) Russia

20. Which one of the following is tallest building of the world?
    (a) Qutub Minar   (b) Eiffel Tower
    (c) Burj Khalifa   (d) Statue of Unity

21. The given building is known as ....

    (a) Statue of Dignity   (b) Statue of Liberty
    (c) Statue of Unity   (d) Statue of Freedom

22. Match the following correctly.

	List I		List II
A.	Gateway of India	1.	Punjab
B.	Jallianwala Bagh	2.	Delhi
C.	Rashtrapati Bhawan	3.	Mumbai

    Codes

	A	B	C		A	B	C
(a)	2	1	3	(b)	3	1	2
(c)	2	3	1	(d)	1	2	3

23. The famous Taj Palace Hotel is located in which city?
    (a) Delhi   (b) Hyderabad
    (c) Mumbai   (d) Calcutta

24. Which of the following is in Karnataka?
    (a) Gateway of India   (b) Konark Sun Temple
    (c) Jantar Mantar   (d) India Gate

Chapter 10

Sun, Moon and Earth

1. Which one of the following is the head of our solar system?
   (a) Sun
   (b) Earth
   (c) Stars
   (d) Moon

2. Which one of the following is the biggest among the given options?
   (a) Moon
   (b) Stars
   (c) Earth
   (d) Sun

3. Which one of the following is given by Sun to us?
   (a) Shade and light
   (b) Heat and darkness
   (c) Heat and light
   (d) Hot and cold

4. In which of the following directions the Sun rises?
   (a) North
   (b) South
   (c) East
   (d) West

5. Which one of the following is true about Sun?
   (a) A Sun is a star
   (b) It has its own heat and light
   (c) It is round in shape
   (d) All of these

6. What is the position of the Earth from the Sun?
   (a) First
   (b) Second
   (c) Third
   (d) Fourth

7. Which one of the following are twinkling in the sky in very large numbers?
   (a) Sun
   (b) Planet
   (c) Moon
   (d) Stars

8. Which of the following is correct?
   (a) The Sun revolves around the Earth.
   (b) The Earth revolves around the Sun.
   (c) The shape of Earth appears to be rectangular.
   (d) Earth is also known as Red planet.

9. What is the other name of our planet Earth?
   (a) The Black Planet
   (b) The Pink Planet
   (c) The Blue Planet
   (d) The Yellow Planet

10. Which one of the following is not in round shape?
    (a) Stars   (b) Moon
    (c) Sun   (d) Earth

11. Find the odd one out.
    (a) Stars   (b) Sun
    (c) Moon   (d) Earth

12. Which type of eclipse occurs when Earth puts a dark shadow on Moon?
    (a) Solar Eclipse   (b) Lunar Eclipse
    (c) Total Eclipse   (d) Partial Eclipse

13. Which one of the following is not found on Earth naturally?
    (a) Mountain   (b) Ocean
    (c) Land   (d) Globe

14. Which one of the following is correct about the Moon?
    (a) The Moon has its own light.   (b) The Moon does not have its own light.
    (c) It is bigger than Earth in size. (d) Both (a) and (b)

15. The Moon revolves around the ....
    (a) Stars   (b) Earth
    (c) Sun   (d) Jupiter

16. The Moon looks brightest during which one of the following phases?
    (a) New Moon   (b) Full Moon
    (c) First Quarter Moon   (d) Third Quarter Moon

17. The Moon looks completely dark during which phase?
    (a) Full Moon   (b) New Moon
    (c) Half Moon   (d) Double Moon

18. What is the correct sequence in according to their size from smallest to biggest?
    (a) Moon < Sun < Earth   (b) Moon < Earth < Sun
    (c) Earth < Moon < Sun   (d) Sun < Moon < Earth

19. Which one of the following is present at the centre of our solar system?
    (a) Stars   (b) Moon
    (c) Earth   (d) Sun

20. The Moon receives light from which of these objects?
    (a) Earth   (b) Sun
    (c) Eclipse   (d) Oceans

Human Body

1. How many sense organs are present in a human body?
   (a) Four
   (b) Five
   (c) Six
   (d) One

2. Which one of the following organs helps us to read books?
   (a) Ears
   (b) Nose
   (c) Mouth
   (d) Eyes

3. Which one of the following parts of human body is uncountable?
   (a) Hands
   (b) Legs
   (c) Hair
   (d) Heart

4. Which of the following activities can you do with your hands?
   (a) Sleeping
   (b) Holding pencil
   (c) Walking
   (d) Running

5. We will use which organ to listen to sound coming from the speakers shown in picture.

   (a) Ears
   (b) Nose
   (c) Hand
   (d) Eyes

6. Which one of the following is not a sense organ in our body?
    (a) Skin   (b) Eyes
    (c) Tongue   (d) Nails

7. Which among the following is also known as storehouse of knowledge in human body?
    (a) Brain   (b) Arms
    (c) Shoulder   (d) Neck

8. The organ shown in the picture will be used by us for which activity?

    (a) Talking to friends   (b) Chewing food
    (c) Sharpening pencil   (d) Washing clothes

9. Which one of the following organs supplies blood to all parts of the body?
    (a) Kidneys   (b) Lungs
    (c) Brain   (d) Heart

10. Our kidney is a ....
    (a) sense organ   (b) external organ
    (c) internal organ   (d) None of these

11. How many lungs are present in a human body?
    (a) Two   (b) Three
    (c) One   (d) Four

12. In which part of the human body the teeth lies?
    (a) In the stomach   (b) In the kidney
    (c) In the mouth   (d) In the legs

13. Which one of the following is not a lower body part?
    (a) Thighs   (b) Neck
    (c) Knees   (d) Toes

14. Which one of the following is the largest organ in human body?
    (a) Hands   (b) Lips
    (c) Kidney   (d) Skin

15. Which of the following organs helps us to digest the food?
    (a) Brain (b) Stomach
    (c) Kidneys (d) Lungs

16. The internal organ helps us in breathing is ....
    (a) lungs (b) mouth
    (c) eyes (d) brain

17. Our .... helps us to taste sweet, sour, bitter and salty things.
    (a) mouth (b) tongue
    (c) nails (d) hands

18. All the other parts of the body work on the instruction of which part of the body?
    (a) Brain (b) Hands
    (c) Hair (d) Lungs

19. Which one of the following parts of body regrow again even when we cut them regularly?
    (a) Nails (b) Hands (c) Tongue (d) Teeth

20. Our nose gives us the sense of ....
    (a) taste (b) smell (c) tongue (d) All of these

21. In which of the following human parts we wear gloves?
    (a) Legs (b) Hands (c) Neck (d) Head

22. The parts of body that are inside us and we cannot see them are called ....
    (a) external organ (b) sense organ
    (c) internal organ (d) None of these

23. Which one of the following is not a part of legs?
    (a) Ankle (b) Knee (c) Toe (d) Shoulder

24. Where shall we wear the item shown in the picture given below.

    (a) Hands (b) Head (c) Legs (d) Shoulder

Animals

1. Which of these animals lives in jungle?
   (a) Lion   (b) Cat
   (c) Dog   (d) Goat

2. Which of these animals does not live in water?
   (a) Dolphin   (b) Octopus
   (c) Fish   (d) Rat

3. Which of the following animals likes to eat carrots?
   (a) Tiger   (b) Dog
   (c) Cat   (d) Rabbit

4. Which of the following birds cannot fly?
   (a) Sparrow   (b) Pigeon
   (c) Parrot   (d) Ostrich

5. Which of the following animals does not have legs?
   (a) Snake   (b) Hen
   (c) Goat   (d) Tiger

6. Which of the following animals can live on both land and water?
   (a) Monkey   (b) Frog
   (c) Fish   (d) Butterfly

7. Match the following.

List I	List II
A. Bird	1. Zebra
B. Insects	2. Cat
C. Pet Animal	3. Peacock
D. Wild Animal	4. Cockroach

Codes

	A	B	C	D			A	B	C	D
(a)	3	4	2	1		(b)	1	2	3	4
(c)	2	3	4	1		(d)	3	4	1	2

8. Which of the following animals does not eat grass?

(a) Cow   (b) Buffalo

(c) Tiger   (d) Goat

9. Match the following animals with their sound.

Animal		Sound
A. Honeybee	1.	Bark
B. Cat	2.	Roar
C. Dog	3.	Buzz
D. Lion	4.	Meow

Codes

	A	B	C	D
(a)	3	4	1	2
(c)	2	3	4	1
(b)	1	2	3	4
(d)	4	3	2	1

10. The animals that lives in forest are known as............ .

(a) wild animals   (b) pet animals

(c) domestic animals   (d) None of these

11. Find the odd one out.

(a) Rat   (b) Butterfly

(c) Honey Bee   (d) Mosquito

12. Match the following.

List I (House)		List II (Animal)
A. Den	1.	Birds
B. Nest	2.	Dog
C. Stable	3.	Lion
D. Kennel	4.	Horse

Codes

	A	B	C	D
(a)	3	1	4	2
(c)	4	3	2	1
(b)	1	2	3	4
(d)	2	3	4	1

13. Which of the following animals lays eggs?

(a) Hen   (b) Cow

(c) Monkey   (d) Rabbit

14. Which of the following animals is shown in the picture?

     (a) Ostrich   (b) Dinosaurs   (c) Snake   (d) Turtle

15. Which of the following animals makes a sound "QUACK QUACK"?
     (a) Hen   (b) Elephant
     (c) Duck   (d) Goat

16. Which of the following animals make Web?
     (a) Honey Bee   (b) Spider   (c) Monkey   (d) Birds

17. Which of the following animal lives in water?
     (a) Whale   (b) Star Fish   (c) Shark   (d) All of these

18. Which of the following is not correctly matched?
     (a) Cat lives – on land   (b) Crocodile lives – in land and water
     (c) Donkey lives – in land and water   (d) Deer lives – on land only

19. Which of the following eat both flesh and plants?

(a)    (b) 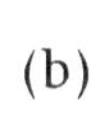

(c) 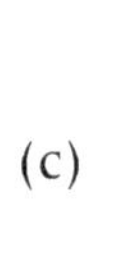   (d) 

20. Which one of the following insects cannot fly?
     (a) Cockroach   (b) Ant
     (c) Butterfly   (d) Both (a) and (b)

21. Which of the following animals is shown in the picture?

(a) Rhinoceros
(c) Spider
(b) Elephant
(d) Bear

22. What is the baby of the cat called?
(a) Puppy
(c) Kitten
(b) Foal
(d) Calf

23. Which one of the following is the fastest animal among the given options?
(a) Snake
(c) Tiger
(b) Elephant
(d) Horse

24. Which of the following birds can see in night clearly?
(a) Sparrow
(c) Pigeon
(b) Owl
(d) None of these

25. Find the odd one out.

(a) 

(b) 

(c) 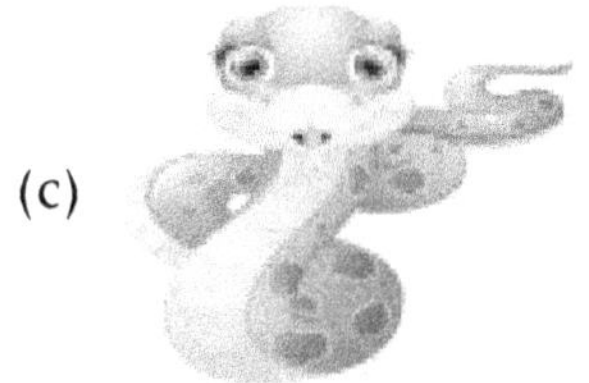

(d) 

Directions (Q. Nos. 26-27) *Name of some animals are given. Find the right answer.*

Tiger, Horse, Fox, Lion, Cow, Goat, Elephant

26. How many animals are known as wild animals ?
(a) 3　　　(b) 4　　　(c) 5　　　(d) 6

27. How many animals are known as domestic animals?
(a) 5　　　(b) 6　　　(c) 2　　　(d) 3

28. Which one of the following is the biggest animal?

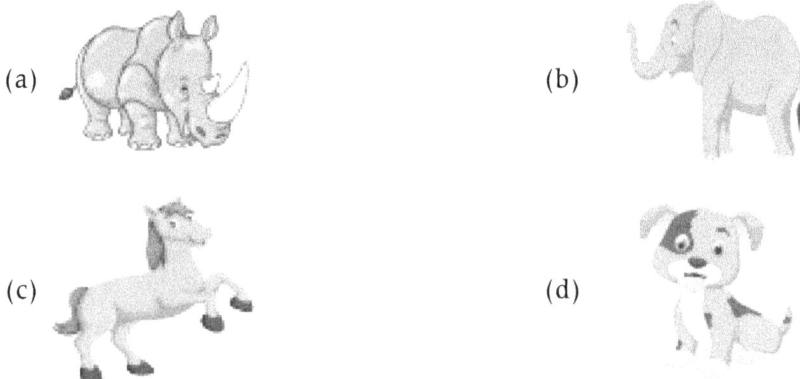

(a)   (b)

(c)   (d)

Directions (Q. Nos. 29-30) *From the given names, count and answer the total number of birds and insects.*

Butterfly , Pigeon, Sparrow, Spider, Frog, Lizard, Bat, Ant, Parrot, Crow

29. How many birds are there in the given names?
(a) 5   (b) 6
(c) 4   (d) 3

30. How many insects are there in the given names?
(a) 6   (b) 7
(c) 5   (d) 8

31. Which one of the following is the smallest animal in the given options?
(a) Rabbit   (b) Squirrel
(c) Ant   (d) Rat

Plants

1. Which one of the following is not a flower?
   (a) Jasmine   (b) Rose   (c) Leave   (d) Marigold

2. Which of the following gives rise to a new plant?
   (a) Root   (b) Seed   (c) Leaves   (d) Stem

3. Which one of the following is not a big and tall plant?
   (a) Banyan tree   (b) Neem tree   (c) Rose plant   (d) Mango tree

4. Which one of the following is not a part of plant?
   (a) Stem   (b) Roots   (c) Leaves   (d) Grass

5. Which one of the following is known as National tree of India?
   (a) Banyan tree   (b) Mango tree   (c) Banana tree   (d) Neem tree

6. Which of the following does we not obtain from plants?
   (a) Cotton   (b) Fruits   (c) Milk   (d) Vegetables

7. Which of the following parts of the plant is always under the soil?
   (a) Leaves   (b) Stem   (c) Roots   (d) Flower

8. Which of the following plants grows only in mud?
   (a) Sunflower   (b) Lotus   (c) Rose   (d) Jasmine

9. Find the odd one out.
   (a) Cucumber   (b) Money plant

   (c) Bottel Gourd   (d) Potato

10. Which of the following can be obtained from a tree?

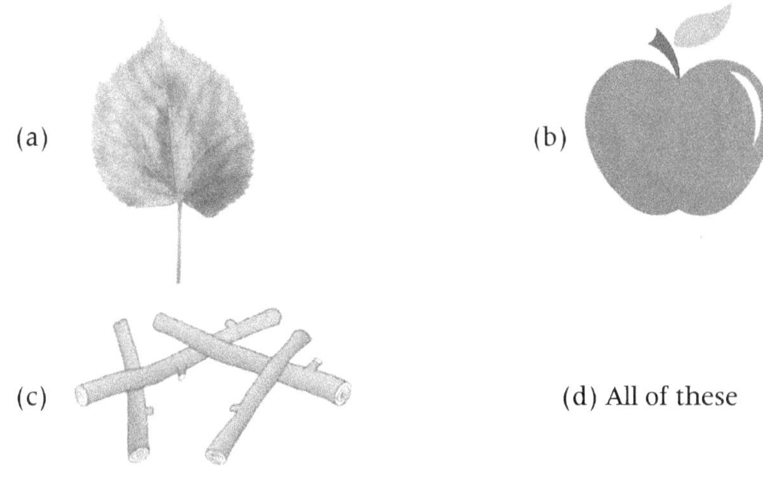

(a)   (b)

(c)   (d) All of these

11. Which of the following plants is used to make medicines?
(a) Tulsi   (b) Orange
(c) Coconut   (d) None of these

12. Which of the following plants is commonly found in desert area?
(a) Sunflower   (b) Money plant
(c) Cactus   (d) Mint

13. We will put .... in the soil to make it a plant.
(a) seeds   (b) grass
(c) roots   (d) leaves

14. Which of the following part of a plant can be eaten by without cooking?
(a) Root   (b) Seeds
(c) Fruits   (d) Leaves

15. .... takes support of walls to grow.
(a) Neem   (b) Grapevine
(c) Potato   (d) Money plant

16. Which one of the following plants is used to make furniture?
(a) Sugarcane   (b) Jasmine
(c) Neem   (d) Bamboo

17. Which of the following things can we obtain from plants?

(a) Mustard Oil

(b) Honey

(c) Milk

(d) Pen

18. Identify the given picture.

(a) Maize

(b) Wheat

(c) Broccoli

(d) Onion

19. Find the odd one out.

(a) Beans

(b) Pulses

(c) Rice

(d) Tomato

Chapter

14

Fruits and Vegetables

1. Which of the following trees gives us fruit?
   (a) Mango Tree   (b) Banyan Tree
   (c) Neem Tree   (d) None of these

2. Find the odd one out.
   (a) Cauliflower   (b) Spinach
   (c) Potato   (d) Banana

3. Which of the following fruits is known as King of Fruits?
   (a) Banana   (b) Mango
   (c) Orange   (d) Apple

4. Which one of the following vegetables can be eaten without cooking?
   (a) Cabbage   (b) Carrot
   (c) Spinach   (d) Beans

5. Which vegetable is shown in the picture given below?

   (a) Ladyfinger   (b) Cabbage
   (c) Spinach   (d) Cauliflower

6. Which of the following fruits is sour in taste?
   (a) Orange   (b) Watermelon
   (c) Banana   (d) Apple

7. Find out the pair of a fruit and a vegetable.
   (a) Mango - Orange
   (b) Papaya - Carrot
   (c) Cabbage - Pears
   (d) Potato - Spinach

8. In which of the following fruits, seeds are not present?
   (a) Watermelon
   (b) Banana
   (c) Papaya
   (d) Apple

9. Which of the following pairs is incorrectly matched?
   (a) Brinjal- Fruit
   (b) Ladyfinger- Vegetable
   (c) Guava - Fruit
   (d) Strawberry- Fruit

10. Find the odd one out.

(a) 

(b) 

(c) 

(d) 

11. Which one of the following fruits is smallest in shape and size?
    (a) Grapes
    (b) Watermelon
    (c) Apple
    (d) Orange

12. I am round in shape. I am pink in colour. Who am I?
    (a) Potato
    (b) Raddish
    (c) Carrot
    (d) Onion

13. Which one of the following is known as King of Vegetables?
    (a) Tomato
    (b) Beans
    (c) Eggplant
    (d) Ladyfinger

14. Which one of the following fruits is given in the picture?

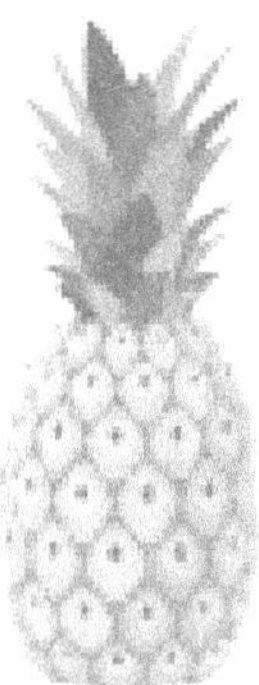

(a) Grapes   (b) Guava
(c) Watermelon   (d) Pineapple

15. Identify the given vegetable.

(a) Cabbage   (b) Broccoli
(c) Spinach   (d) None of these

Computers

1. Which one of the following parts of computer is used to type letters and numbers?
   (a) Mouse   (b) Monitor
   (c) Printer   (d) Keyboard

2. Which one of the following is not a part of computer?
   (a) Keyboard   (b) Monitor
   (c) CPU   (d) CD

3. The parts of computer shown in the picture below can be used for doing which activity?

   (a) Watch cartoons   (b) Play games
   (c) Listen music   (d) Write your name

4. Which one of the following equipments will we use while doing video call on computer?
   (a) Printer   (b) Scanner
   (c) Webcam   (d) Mouse

5. Which of these is not part of a computer?

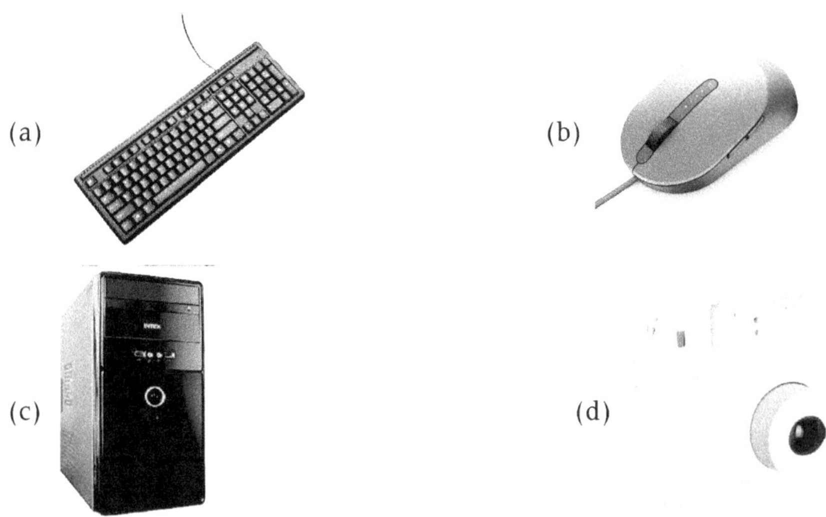

(a)   (b)

(c)   (d)

6. Which one of the following is used to print the document on paper?
   (a) Printer   (b) Mouse
   (c) Headphone   (d) Monitor

7. Identify the given part of the computer.

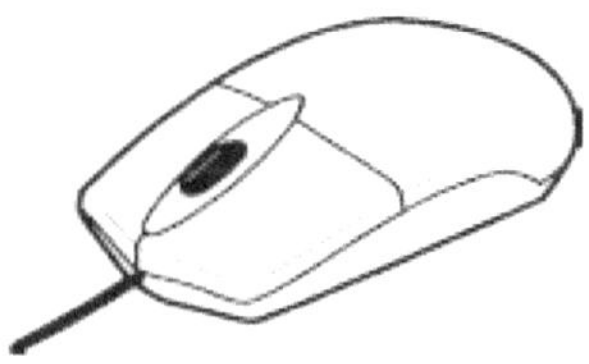

   (a) Mouse   (b) Monitor
   (c) Headphone   (d) CPU

8. Which of the following is used to listen to sound in the ear?
   (a) Monitor   (b) Joystick
   (c) Headphone   (d) Mouse

9. Which one of the following key is not present in the keyboard?
   (a) Caps lock keys   (b) Number Keys
   (c) Direction keys   (d) Alphabet keys

10. Which of the following activities we cannot do on computer?
    (a) Painting   (b) Swimming
    (c) Playing games   (d) Watching cartoons

11. Which one of the following is called as the brain of computer?
   (a) Monitor   (b) Mouse
   (c) Keyboard   (d) CPU

12. How many buttons does the mouse have?
   (a) One   (b) Two
   (c) Three   (d) Four

13. Which one of the following search engine is used to search on internet?
   (a) Facebook   (b) Google
   (c) Whatsapp   (d) Instagram

14. Which one of the following is stored by computer?
   (a) Food   (b) Clothes
   (c) Data   (d) All of these

15. Which one of the following parts of computer is attached to CPU?
   (a) Mouse   (b) Keyboard
   (c) Monitor   (d) All of these

16. The part of computer shown in the picture can be used to do which activity?

   (a) Listen Music   (b) Click Photos
   (c) Watch Pictures   (d) Make Calls

Important Days

1. Which one of the following days is celebrated on 26th January every year?
   - (a) Independence Day
   - (b) Republic Day
   - (c) Teacher's Day
   - (d) Mother's Day

2. Which of the following days is celebrated on 14th November every year?
   - (a) Children's Day
   - (b) Teacher's Day
   - (c) Independence Day
   - (d) Holi

3. On which of the following dates our Independence Day is celebrated every year?
   - (a) 15th June
   - (b) 15th July
   - (c) 25th December
   - (d) 15th August

4. Which of the following days is celebrated on the date 25th in December every year?
   - (a) Christmas
   - (b) Holi
   - (c) Diwali
   - (d) Gandhi Jayanti

5. On which of the following dates the Teacher's Day is celebrated every year?
   - (a) 1st September
   - (b) 1st October
   - (c) 5th September
   - (d) 31st October

6. Which of the following days is celebrated on 21st of June?
   - (a) World Environment Day
   - (b) World Health Day
   - (c) International Yoga Day
   - (d) International Earth's Day

7. On the birthday's occasion of which of the following, Teacher's Day is celebrated?
   - (a) A.P.J Abdul Kalam
   - (b) Mahatma Gandhi
   - (c) Sarvepalli Radhakrishnan
   - (d) Jawaharlal Nehru

8. Which of the following days is celebrated on 22nd April every year?
   - (a) Earth's Day
   - (b) Yoga Day
   - (c) Environment Day
   - (d) Milk Day

9. On which of the following date Environment Day is celebrated every year?
   - (a) 5th June
   - (b) 5th July
   - (c) 5th August
   - (d) 5th December

10. Our national festival Gandhi Jayanti is celebrated on............. .
    (a) 2nd October   (b) 2nd August
    (c) 1st January   (d) 31st December

11. On which of the following days, our Prime Minister hoists the national flag on Red Fort?
    (a) Independence Day   (b) Republic Day
    (c) Gandhi Jayanti   (d) Diwali

12. The birthday date of our first Prime Minister is celebrated as.......... .
    (a) Mother's Day   (b) Teacher's Day
    (c) Children's Day   (d) Christmas Day

13. What do we on the occasion of Environment Day in our school?
    (a) Plant trees in our school   (b) Takes holiday
    (c) Play cricket   (d) Make new friends

14. The 2nd October is celebrated worldwide as............ .
    (a) International Milk Day   (b) International Water Day
    (c) International Yoga Day   (d) International Day of Non-violence

Sports

1. In which game would you score a century?
   (a) Football   (b) Hockey   (c) Cricket   (d) Badminton

2. The FIFA World Cup is related to which of the following sports?
   (a) Football   (b) Chess   (c) Cricket   (d) Volleyball

3. Which of these sports do you play with a shuttlecock?
   (a) Table Tennis   (b) Hockey   (c) Ludo   (d) Badminton

4. Which one of the following is not an indoor game?
   (a) Volleyball   (b) Chess
   (c) Carrom   (d) Snake and Ladder

5. The sports person shown in the image plays which sports?

   (a) Cricket   (b) Football
   (c) Hockey   (d) Tennis

6. What is the name of the sports person shown in the image?

   (a) Saina Nehwal   (b) PV Sindhu
   (c) Sania Mirza   (d) Hima Das

7. Which of the following games is played with curved stick and a ball?
   (a) Hockey   (b) Volleyball
   (c) Football   (d) Cricket

8. Which of the following equipments is used while doing Cycling?
   (a) Helmet   (b) Cricket Pads
   (c) Boxing Gloves   (d) None of these

9. Which one of the following is an indoor game?
   (a) Table Tennis   (b) Golf
   (c) Cricket   (d) Football

10. The given kit is used in which of the following sports?

   (a) Golf   (b) Cricket
   (c) Badminton   (d) Carrom

11. What is the name of an indoor game in which participants swim in water?
   (a) Swimming   (b) Running
   (c) Shooting   (d) Racing

12. The game of Cricket is played on ....
   (a) nets   (b) pitch
   (c) water   (d) None of these

13. In which of the following sports participants hit the target by using air guns?
   (a) Racing   (b) Hockey
   (c) Swimming   (d) Shooting

14. In which of the following country does the game of Chess originated?
   (a) India   (b) China
   (c) USA   (d) Russia

15. The famous sportsperson Saina Nehwal is related to which of the following sports?
   (a) Cricket   (b) Badminton
   (c) Hockey   (d) Chess

Current Affairs

1. Who is the current President of India?
   (a) Ram Nath Kovind
   (b) Pratibha Patil
   (c) Pranab Mukherjee
   (d) Shankar Dayal Sharma

2. Who is the current Prime Minister of India?
   (a) Manmohan Singh
   (b) Narendra Modi
   (c) Atal Bihari Vajpayee
   (d) L K Gujral

3. Nike is the brand of ....
   (a) Chocolate
   (b) Shoes
   (c) Computers
   (d) Books

4. Who is Miss India 2020?
   (a) Manushi Chillar
   (b) Manasa Varanasi
   (c) Sushmita Sen
   (d) Priyanka Chopra

5. Which film features a wolf named Akeera and a black panther named Bagheera?
   (a) Doremon
   (b) Pokemon
   (c) The Jungle Book
   (d) Chota Bheem

6. Who is the current Chief Minister of Delhi?
   (a) Arvind Kejriwal
   (b) Kiran Bedi
   (c) Sheila Dikshit
   (d) Sushma Swaraj

7. Which among the following is not a news channel
   (a) India Today
   (b) Aaj Tak
   (c) NDTV
   (d) Colors

8. The campaign to promote cleanliness in our environment is ....
   (a) Make in India
   (b) Startup India
   (c) Swachch Bharat Abhiyan
   (d) None of these

9. Which actor is popularly known as king Khan?
   (a) Salman Khan
   (b) Amir Khan
   (c) Shahrukh Khan
   (d) Irfan Khan

10. The pandemic due to which lockdown was imposed is known as ....
    (a) COVID-19
    (b) Coronashield
    (c) Covaxin
    (d) Corona illness

PRACTICE SET 01

1. Rajiv is the brother of my mother. How Rajiv is related to me?
   (a) Uncle
   (b) Maternal Uncle
   (c) Cousin
   (d) Nephew

2. Who will you call to your house when you want to repair water taps and pipes?
   (a) Carpenter
   (b) Blacksmith
   (c) Cobbler
   (d) Plumber

3. Which of the following habits help us to remain healthy and fit?
   (a) Doing exercise
   (b) Eating junk food
   (c) Sleeping 14 hours a day
   (d) Playing games on computer for 6 hours

4. Which one of the following is not a Union Territory of India?
   (a) Ladakh
   (b) Tripura
   (c) Lakshadweep
   (d) Chandigarh

5. The Traditional dress shown in the picture belongs to which state?
   (a) Rajasthan
   (b) Gujarat
   (c) Kerala
   (d) Assam

6. Name the famous monument which is located in Hyderabad?
   (a) Jantar Mantar
   (b) Sanchi Stupa
   (c) Qutub Minar
   (d) Char Minar

7. The famous slogan "Give me blood I will give you freedom" was given by......... .
   (a) Subhas Chandra Bose
   (b) Rabindranath Tagore
   (c) Sardar Patel
   (d) Chandra Shekhar Azad

8. Which of the following fairs held in Prayagraj?
   (a) Kumbh Mela
   (b) Pushkar Mela
   (c) Craft Mela
   (d) None of these

9. Which one of the following is our national tree?
   (a) The Banana Tree
   (b) The Banyan Tree
   (c) The Neem Tree
   (d) The Mango Tree

10. The Sun is at the center of solar system and also known as ....
    (a) head of the solar system
    (b) principal of the solar system
    (c) father of solar system
    (d) None of these

11. Which one of the following parts of human body is used in chewing and tearing the food?
    (a) Legs
    (b) Arms
    (c) Teeth
    (d) Nose

12. Which one of the following animals lives in Kennel?
    (a) Fox
    (b) Bear
    (c) Tiger
    (d) Dog

13. The root is always found ....
    (a) inside the soil
    (b) outside the soil
    (c) in the leaves
    (d) None of these

14. Which one of the following fruits is biggest in size?
    (a) Banana
    (b) Apple
    (c) Orange
    (d) Watermelon

15. Which of the following activities can be done by using computer?
    (a) Painting
    (b) Running
    (c) Walking
    (d) Sleeping

16. Which one of the following dates is celebrated as Environment's Day?
    (a) 21st June
    (b) 12th June
    (c) 5th June
    (d) 10th June

17. Which one of the following is associated with Indian cricket team?
    (a) Jasprit Bumrah
    (b) Sunil Chhetri
    (c) Sushil Kumar
    (d) Anup Kumar

18. Which of the following helps us to repairs our cars and motorbikes?
    (a) Chemist
    (b) Mechanic
    (c) Carpenter
    (d) Doctor

19. Which of the following is a small family?
    (a) Parents and one child
    (b) Grandparents, parents and three children
    (c) Grandparents, parents and uncle aunt
    (d) None of these

20. In which of the following places doctors and nurses take care of the sick and injured person?
    (a) Library
    (b) Restaurants
    (c) Hospital
    (d) Post office

21. What will you do when your relatives come to your home?
    (a) Ignore them
    (b) Wish them with happiness
    (c) Go outside and play
    (d) Sleep

22. Find the mismatched.
    (a) Northern state – Jammu and Kashmir   (b) Southern state – Karnataka
    (c) Eastern state – Madhya Pradesh   (d) Western state – Gujarat

23. Vada Pav and Misal Pav is famous in which of the following states?
    (a) Gujarat   (b) Rajasthan
    (c) Himachal Pradesh   (d) Maharashtra

24. Identify the given famous building.

    (a) The Burj Khalifa   (b) Time Square   (c) Statue of Unity   (d) The Big Ben

25. The national leader Bhim Rao Ambedkar is popularly known as
    (a) Baba Saheb   (b) Neta ji   (c) Iron Man of India   (d) Mahatma

26. In which of the following festivals a national parade is organised on India Gate every year?
    (a) Republic Day   (b) Independence Day
    (c) Eid   (d) Dusshera

27. The strip of the National Flag marked in the picture will be of which colour?

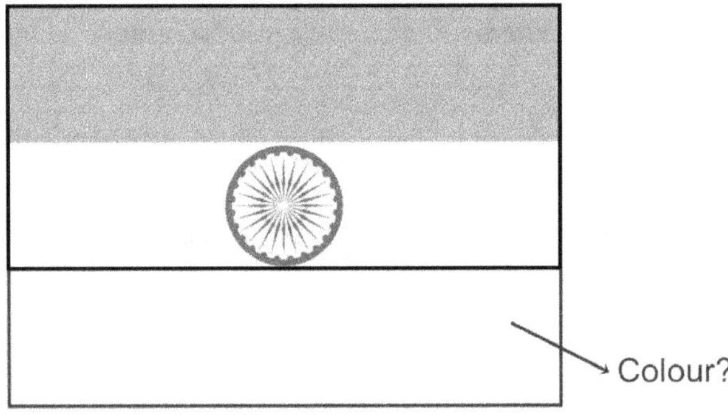

    (a) Blue   (b) Green   (c) Yellow   (d) Pink

28. Which of the following is the only planet where life exists?
    (a) Earth   (b) Uranus   (c) Sun   (d) Mercury

29. Which sense organ will be used to smell the fragrance of flowers shown in the image?

    (a) Tongue   (b) Nose   (c) Skin   (d) Ears

30. The Cow and Buffalo are the ....
    (a) Wild Animals   (b) Domestic Animals   (c) Insects   (d) Birds

31. Which of the following plant grows in water and known as a aquatic plant?
    (a) Lotus   (b) Rose   (c) Marigold   (d) Sunflower

32. Which one of the following vegetables is red in colour?
    (a) Brinjal   (b) Pumpkin   (c) Carrot   (d) Ladyfinger

33. Which of the following is not a part of computer?
    (a) Mouse   (b) Monitor   (c) Pen drive   (d) CPU

34. On which of the following days the National Flag is hoisted in our school?
    (a) Independence Day   (b) Diwali
    (c) Christmas   (d) Navratri

35. The equipments shown in the image given below are used to play which sports?

    (a) Tennis   (b) Kho Kho   (c) Badminton   (d) Cricket

PRACTICE SET 02

1. Find the odd one out.
   (a) Diwali
   (b) Holi
   (c) Rakshabandhan
   (d) Eid

2. In which of the following places, you go to buy vegetables and fruits?
   (a) School
   (b) Park
   (c) Restaurant
   (d) Market

3. Which one of the following is not a bad manner?
   (a) Shouting in the class
   (b) Throwing garbage in parks
   (c) Talking while doing dinner
   (d) Respect the elders

4. Which one of the following is not a state in India?
   (a) Sikkim
   (b) Puducherry
   (c) Uttarakhand
   (d) Karnataka

5. Identify the national animal of India shown in the picture.

   (a) Lion
   (b) Leopard
   (c) Bengal Tiger
   (d) Giraffe

6. Which one of the following freedom fighter gave the slogan 'Do or Die'?
   (a) Subhas Chandra Bose
   (b) Jawaharlal Nehru
   (c) Mahatma Gandhi
   (d) Bhagat Singh

7. Which one of the festivals is known as festival of lights?
   (a) Dusshera
   (b) Holi
   (c) Diwali
   (d) Eid

8. Which of the following drinks is famous in the state Punjab?
   (a) Pepsi   (b) Tea   (c) Lassi
   (d) Coffee

9. Identify the person with the help of the uniform given in the picture.

   (a) Postman   (b) Policeman   (c) Armyman   (d) Doctor

10. From the given options, which of the following is smallest in the size?
    (a) Earth   (b) Sun   (c) Moon   (d) Universe

11. Which of the following sense organs of human body helps us to taste the food?
    (a) Mouth   (b) Tongue   (c) Eyes   (d) Ears

12. Which one of the following animals cannot live without water?
    (a) Snake   (b) Crocodile   (c) Turtle   (d) Fish

13. Match the following.

	List I		List II
A.	Onion	1.	Grain
B.	Watermelon	2.	Flower
C.	Jasmine	3.	Fruit
D.	Barley	4.	Vegetable

    Codes

	A	B	C	D			A	B	C	D
(a)	1	2	3	4		(b)	4	3	2	1
(c)	3	4	1	2		(d)	2	3	4	1

14. Which of the following we cannot obtain from plants?
    (a) Grains   (b) Flowers   (c) Honey   (d) Fruits

15. The computer part shown in the picture can be used for which purpose?

(a) Watch movies   (b) Listen songs
(c) Type your name   (d) Click on screen

16. Which of the following dates is celebrated as Earth's Day every year?
(a) 1st January   (b) 31st December   (c) 18th April   (d) 22nd April

17. In which of the following sports will you check and mate to the opponent?
(a) Cricket   (b) Ludo   (c) Chess   (d) Volleyball

18. Which of the following organs of our body, we cannot touch generally?
(a) Hands   (b) Kidney   (c) Nails   (d) Chest

19. Nikita is the sister of my brother. Nikita is my ....
(a) Mother   (b) Brother   (c) Sister   (d) Daughter

20. Which one of the following arrest criminals and keep the city safe from thieves?
(a) Armyman   (b) Doctor   (c) Policeman   (d) Carpenter

21. Which one of the following good habits should be done daily?
(a) Cutting the nails   (b) Comb hairs   (c) Cutting the hairs   (d) Tear the clothes

22. Which one of the following states is located in Southern India?
(a) Jammu and Kashmir   (b) Himachal Pradesh
(c) Punjab   (d) Tamil Nadu

23. The given symbol is the symbol of our ....

(a) Emblem   (b) Rupee   (c) Bird   (d) Motto

24. Our former Prime Minister Lal Bahadur Shastri is also known as............ .
(a) Sardar   (b) Guruji   (c) Bapu ji   (d) Man of Peace

25. Which community goes to worship at the place shown in the image?

    (a) Hindu   (b) Muslim   (c) Sikhs   (d) Christian

26. The famous monument Taj Mahal is located in which of the following states?
    (a) Madhya Pradesh   (b) Karnataka   (c) Punjab   (d) Uttar Pradesh

27. Which of the famous buildings is located in Paris, France?
    (a) Statue of Liberty   (b) Statue of Unity   (c) Eiffel Tower   (d) Red Fort

28. The Earth is on the third position from the ....
    (a) Moon   (b) Venus   (c) Mars   (d) Sun

29. The internal organ of our body helps us in taking decisions is............. .
    (a) stomach   (b) head   (c) brain   (d) kidney

30. Which one of the following animals make a sound 'HISS'?
    (a) Duck   (c) Pigeon   (c) Snake   (d) Deer

31. Which of the following is not a fruit?
    (a) Marigold   (b) Grapes   (c) Mango   (d) Pineapple

32. Which one of the following statements is correct?
    (a) Mango is a vegetable   (b) Brinjal is a vegetable
    (c) Apple is a vegetable   (d) Banana is a vegetable

33. How many alphabets keys are present in the keyboard?
    (a) 20   (b) 22   (c) 24   (d) 26

34. Which of the following days is celebrated on 2nd day of October?
    (a) Diwali   (b) Environment Day   (c) Republic Day   (d) Gandhi Jayanti

35. The famous sports personality PV Sindhu is related to which of the following sports?
    (a) Tennis   (b) Hockey   (c) Basketballs   (d) Badminton

Answers

Chapter 1   Me and My Family

1. (d)	**2.** (c)	**3.** (b)	**4.** (b)	**5.** (a)	**6.** (b)	**7.** (d)	**8.** (b)	**9.** (d)	**10.** (b)
11. (a)	**12.** (d)	**13.** (a)	**14.** (c)	**15.** (d)	**16.** (a)	**17.** (a)	**18.** (b)	**19.** (c)	**20.** (d)
21. (a)	**22.** (c)								

Chapter 2   Our Surroundings

1. (c)	**2.** (a)	**3.** (c)	**4.** (a)	**5.** (a)	**6.** (b)	**7.** (b)	**8.** (b)	**9.** (c)	**10.** (d)
11. (c)	**12.** (a)	**13.** (d)	**14.** (c)	**15.** (a)	**16.** (c)	**17.** (b)	**18.** (a)	**19.** (a)	**20.** (d)

Chapter 3   Good Habits and Manners

1. (d)	**2.** (d)	**3.** (b)	**4.** (c)	**5.** (b)	**6.** (d)	**7.** (d)	**8.** (d)	**9.** (b)	**10.** (d)
11. (c)	**12.** (c)	**13.** (d)	**14.** (d)	**15.** (c)	**16.** (a)	**17.** (d)			

Chapter 4   My Country

1. (b)	**2.** (b)	**3.** (c)	**4.** (d)	**5.** (a)	**6.** (c)	**7.** (c)	**8.** (b)	**9.** (a)	**10.** (c)
11. (b)	**12.** (d)	**13.** (a)	**14.** (a)	**15.** (a)	**16.** (a)	**17.** (a)	**18.** (c)	**19.** (c)	**20.** (d)
21. (c)	**22.** (a)	**23.** (b)							

Chapter 5   Our National Symbols

1. (d)	**2.** (c)	**3.** (c)	**4.** (b)	**5.** (a)	**6.** (b)	**7.** (a)	**8.** (b)	**9.** (a)	**10.** (a)
11. (a)	**12.** (b)	**13.** (a)	**14.** (d)	**15.** (b)					

Chapter 6   Our Freedom Fighters and National Leaders

1. (b)	**2.** (d)	**3.** (a)	**4.** (b)	**5.** (c)	**6.** (d)	**7.** (d)	**8.** (a)	**9.** (a)	**10.** (a)
11. (c)	**12.** (a)	**13.** (d)	**14.** (b)	**15.** (b)	**16.** (d)	**17.** (c)	**18.** (b)		

Chapter 7   Fairs, Festivals and Religions

1. (d)	**2.** (b)	**3.** (c)	**4.** (a)	**5.** (c)	**6.** (a)	**7.** (a)	**8.** (d)	**9.** (b)	**10.** (b)
11. (d)	**12.** (b)	**13.** (a)	**14.** (c)	**15.** (a)	**16.** (b)	**17.** (d)	**18.** (d)	**19.** (d)	**20.** (d)
21. (c)	**22.** (a)								

Chapter 8   Dress and Food

1. (a)	**2.** (a)	**3.** (a)	**4.** (c)	**5.** (a)	**6.** (a)	**7.** (a)	**8.** (c)	**9.** (d)	**10.** (b)
11. (d)	**12.** (b)	**13.** (d)	**14.** (b)	**15.** (d)					

Chapter 9   Famous Buildings and Monuments

1. (b)	**2.** (c)	**3.** (b)	**4.** (a)	**5.** (c)	**6.** (a)	**7.** (c)	**8.** (a)	**9.** (b)	**10.** (a)
11. (c)	**12.** (d)	**13.** (a)	**14.** (a)	**15.** (d)	**16.** (b)	**17.** (b)	**18.** (a)	**19.** (c)	**20.** (c)
21. (b)	**22.** (b)	**23.** (c)	**24.** (b)						

Chapter 10   Sun, Moon and Earth

1. (a)	**2.** (d)	**3.** (c)	**4.** (c)	**5.** (d)	**6.** (c)	**7.** (d)	**8.** (b)	**9.** (c)	**10.** (a)
11. (a)	**12.** (b)	**13.** (d)	**14.** (b)	**15.** (b)	**16.** (b)	**17.** (d)	**18.** (b)	**19.** (d)	**20.** (b)

Chapter 11   Human Body

1. (b)	**2.** (d)	**3.** (c)	**4.** (b)	**5.** (a)	**6.** (d)	**7.** (a)	**8.** (b)	**9.** (d)	**10.** (c)
11. (a)	**12.** (c)	**13.** (b)	**14.** (d)	**15.** (b)	**16.** (a)	**17.** (b)	**18.** (a)	**19.** (a)	**20.** (b)
21. (b)	**22.** (c)	**23.** (d)	**24.** (c)						

Chapter 12   Animals

1. (a)	**2.** (d)	**3.** (d)	**4.** (d)	**5.** (a)	**6.** (b)	**7.** (a)	**8.** (c)	**9.** (a)	**10.** (a)
11. (a)	**12.** (a)	**13.** (a)	**14.** (d)	**15.** (c)	**16.** (b)	**17.** (d)	**18.** (c)	**19.** (d)	**20.** (b)
21. (a)	**22.** (c)	**23.** (c)	**24.** (b)	**25.** (a)	**26.** (b)	**27.** (d)	**28.** (b)	**29.** (c)	**30.** (a)
31. (c)									

Chapter 13   Plants

1. (c)	**2.** (b)	**3.** (c)	**4.** (d)	**5.** (a)	**6.** (c)	**7.** (c)	**8.** (b)	**9.** (b)	**10.** (d)
11. (a)	**12.** (c)	**13.** (a)	**14.** (c)	**15.** (b)	**16.** (d)	**17.** (a)	**18.** (a)	**19.** (d)	

Chapter 14   Fruits and Vegetables

1. (a)	**2.** (d)	**3.** (b)	**4.** (b)	**5.** (d)	**6.** (a)	**7.** (b)	**8.** (b)	**9.** (a)	**10.** (c)
11. (a)	**12.** (d)	**13.** (c)	**14.** (d)	**15.** (b)					

Chapter 15   Computers

1. (d)	**2.** (d)	**3.** (c)	**4.** (c)	**5.** (d)	**6.** (a)	**7.** (a)	**8.** (c)	**9.** (c)	**10.** (b)
11. (d)	**12.** (b)	**13.** (b)	**14.** (c)	**15.** (d)	**16.** (c)				

Chapter 16   Important Days

1. (b)	**2.** (a)	**3.** (d)	**4.** (a)	**5.** (c)	**6.** (c)	**7.** (c)	**8.** (a)	**9.** (a)	**10.** (a)
11. (a)	**12.** (c)	**13.** (a)	**14.** (d)						

Chapter 17   Sports

1. (c)	**2.** (a)	**3.** (d)	**4.** (a)	**5.** (a)	**6.** (c)	**7.** (a)	**8.** (a)	**9.** (a)	**10.** (a)
11. (a)	**12.** (b)	**13.** (d)	**14.** (a)	**15.** (b)					

Chapter 18   Current Affairs

1. (a)	**2.** (b)	**3.** (b)	**4.** (b)	**5.** (c)	**6.** (a)	**7.** (d)	**8.** (c)	**9.** (c)	**10.** (a)

Practice Set 1

1. (b)	**2.** (d)	**3.** (a)	**4.** (b)	**5.** (c)	**6.** (d)	**7.** (a)	**8.** (a)	**9.** (b)	**10.** (a)
11. (c)	**12.** (d)	**13.** (a)	**14.** (d)	**15.** (a)	**16.** (c)	**17.** (a)	**18.** (b)	**19.** (a)	**20.** (c)
21. (b)	**22.** (c)	**23.** (d)	**24.** (d)	**25.** (a)	**26.** (a)	**27.** (b)	**28.** (a)	**29.** (b)	**30.** (b)
31. (a)	**32.** (c)	**33.** (c)	**34.** (a)	**35.** (c)					

Practice Set 2

1. (d)	**2.** (d)	**3.** (d)	**4.** (b)	**5.** (c)	**6.** (c)	**7.** (c)	**8.** (c)	**9.** (a)	**10.** (c)
11. (b)	**12.** (d)	**13.** (b)	**14.** (c)	**15.** (c)	**16.** (d)	**17.** (c)	**18.** (b)	**19.** (c)	**20.** (c)
21. (b)	**22.** (d)	**23.** (b)	**24.** (d)	**25.** (d)	**26.** (d)	**27.** (c)	**28.** (d)	**29.** (c)	**30.** (c)
31. (a)	**32.** (b)	**33.** (d)	**34.** (d)	**35.** (d)